Benji's Computer Bug

Story by Cameron Macintosh
Illustrations by Carissa Harris

Text: Cameron Macintosh
Publishers: Tania Mazzeo and Eliza Webb
Series consultant: Amanda Sutera
  Hands on Heads Consulting
Editor: Beth Browne
Project editor: Annabel Smith
Designer: Jess Kelly
Project designer: Danielle Maccarone
Illustrations: Carissa Harris
Production controller: Renee Tome

NovaStar

Text © 2024 Cengage Learning Australia Pty Limited
Illustrations © 2024 Cengage Learning Australia Pty Limited

Copyright Notice
This Work is copyright. No part of this Work may be reproduced, stored
in a retrieval system, or transmitted in any form or by any means
without prior written permission of the Publisher. Except as permitted
under the *Copyright Act 1968*, for example any fair dealing for the
purposes of private study, research, criticism or review, subject to
certain limitations. These limitations include: Restricting the copying to a
maximum of one chapter or 10% of this book, whichever is greater;
Providing an appropriate notice and warning with the copies of the
Work disseminated; Taking all reasonable steps to limit access to these
copies to people authorised to receive these copies; Ensuring you hold
the appropriate Licences issued by the Copyright Agency Limited ("CAL"),
supply a remuneration notice to CAL and pay any required fees.

ISBN 978 0 17 033412 9

Cengage Learning Australia
Level 5, 80 Dorcas Street
Southbank VIC 3006 Australia
Phone: 1300 790 853
Email: aust.nelsonprimary@cengage.com

For learning solutions, visit **cengage.com.au**

Printed in China by 1010 Printing International Ltd
1 2 3 4 5 6 7 28 27 26 25 24

*Nelson acknowledges the Traditional Owners and Custodians
of the lands of all First Nations Peoples. We pay respect
to Elders past and present, and extend that respect to
all First Nations Peoples today.*

Contents

Chapter 1

The Coding Competition

The students of class 4S hurried to their desks at the end of lunch. It was time for their coding class, and they were all very excited. Over the last few months, their teacher, Ms Samara, had been teaching them how to write computer code to make their own games and apps.

"Coding means writing instructions to tell a computer to do a task," she had told them in the first class. "Look at this code on the whiteboard."

To most of the class, the code looked like a strange pattern of words, letters and numbers. But before long, they were writing code to make apps of their own.

The class listened as Ms Samara said, "I have an announcement. You've all been doing incredibly well with your coding ... so we're going to have a competition! You can all show each other how much you've learnt."

Benji smiled and glanced over at Harper, just as Harper glanced at him. Harper and Benji were the two best students in the class at coding. In a few short months, they'd both made some exciting apps.

Benji had made an app that allowed him to feed his goldfish from any place at any time.

Harper had made an app to track what her dog was eating.

Ms Samara continued: "Your task is to create an app that will be useful in the classroom. You have two weeks, and then everyone will present their app to the class."

"Is there a prize for the winner?" asked Harper, excitedly.

"Yes," replied Ms Samara. "The winner gets to visit a video game studio and have a coding lesson with the people who design the games."

"That sounds amazing!" said Harper.

Benji was excited, too. He loved coding more than anything. At home, he loved watching online videos to learn more about it. He really wanted to write code for video games when he was older.

I'd learn so much from visiting a game studio, Benji thought to himself. *I can't let Harper win.*

Chapter 2

Benji's Big Idea

Over the next two weeks, everyone worked hard on writing code for their apps.

Benji had decided to make an app to water the classroom plants. Harper was making an app to control the ceiling fan from anywhere in the classroom.
Each day, the kids would test their apps and work on improving them. It was challenging, but they all enjoyed it.

Benji's app was working well, but as the presentation day approached, he kept a close eye on Harper's progress. Her app seemed to be getting better every single day.

"You're doing a great job, Harper," said Ms Samara.

"Thanks," Harper replied. "But it's still a bit slow. I wish the fan would spin at the same time as I draw circles on my tablet."

Hmmm, Benji thought to himself. *Harper has just given me an idea. I think I know how I can make sure she doesn't win the competition.*

Benji spent every spare moment of the next weekend at his computer, writing special code. The code was for a computer bug for Harper's app to make the ceiling fan spin out of control!

As soon as he was finished, Benji sent Harper an email with the code attached.

Hey, Harper!

I noticed that your app has been running slowly. Here's some code I've written to make apps faster. You can use it too.

See you tomorrow!

Benji

 App.code

That night, Harper wrote back to him.

Thanks, Benji. That's very cool of you!

Deep down, Benji knew what he had done wasn't right. But he wanted to win more than anything.

Chapter 3

Code Chaos

The presentation day finally arrived. Each student showed their code on the whiteboard before demonstrating how their app worked. First up was Rina. Her app was supposed to help Ms Samara control the interactive whiteboard. It turned the whiteboard on and off, but it didn't do much else.

Next was Harper. Benji smirked as she stood up in front of the class. As soon as she tapped on the tablet to start her app, the fan spun around so fast it went blurry. There was nothing she could do to stop it. Harper's eyes widened in shock as Ms Samara hurried over to the wall switch and turned the fan off.

"This has never happened before!" cried Harper. "I don't know what's gone wrong."

Finally, it was Benji's turn to present his app. He tapped on the tablet, and a tube began to drip water onto a plant by the windowsill. Benji smiled, but as he tapped the tablet again, water spurted out fast over the next plant and onto the floor.

Suddenly, the whiteboard screen started to fill with letters and numbers. More and more lines of code flashed onto the whiteboard, including the code he'd written to ruin Harper's app.

Oh no! Benji thought. *The bug's messing up my app, too!*

The class crowded around the whiteboard and read the code. It didn't take them long to realise what Benji had done.

"I'm very disappointed, Benji," said Ms Samara. "I have to disqualify you from the competition. And you need to remove this bug from Harper's app. Everyone else can present their apps again next week."

"I'm sorry, Harper," said Benji. "You know how much I love coding. I really wanted to go to the video game studio."

"We all wanted the prize," said Harper, "but the rest of us didn't cheat to try to get it."

appbug

"fastfan"

Chapter 4

Harper's Handshake

A week later, Benji watched sadly as everyone else demonstrated their apps again. This time, Harper's app worked perfectly. She was able to make the fan move in time with her fingertip as she drew circles on her tablet.

"I've come to a decision," said Ms Samara, after all the presentations were complete. "The winner is ... Harper!"

Everyone clapped and congratulated Harper. Even Benji was impressed.

That lunchtime, Benji noticed Harper
following him outside.

"I guess you're here to remind me what
a terrible cheat I am," he said to her.

"Actually," she said, "I think you're really
clever at coding. Your trick gave me an
idea. We could start our own coding club
and share our ideas with each other.
We learnt so much
during the competition.
Imagine what we could
achieve together."

Benji couldn't quite believe what he was hearing. "That sounds great," he said. "Thanks, Harper!"

"Just one thing," said Harper, shaking Benji's hand. "Promise me you'll leave the bugs outside?"

"That's a promise!" laughed Benji.